UNDER THE COVERS
THE NAKED TRUTH ABOUT SEXUAL HEALTH

Rebecca M Cooke

Copyright © 2025 Rebecca M Cooke

All rights reserved.

No part of this book may be reproduced in any form or by any electronic or mechanical means including information storage and retrieval systems, without permission in writing from the Publisher.

Publishers:
Inspiring Publishers
PO box 159 Calwell ACT 2905, Australia.
Email: inspiringpublishers@gmail.com

A catalogue record for this book is available from the National Library of Australia

National Library of Australia Prepublication Data Service

Author: Rebecca M Cooke

Title: **UNDER THE COVERS: The Naked Truth About Sexual Health**

ISBN: 978-1-923449-13-8 (Print)

ISBN: 978-1-923449-14-5 (ePub2)

INTRODUCTION

Unlock the secrets to a happier, healthier, and more fulfilling intimate life in this comprehensive guide to sexual health and wellness. Written by a seasoned adult shop manager who has heard it all, this book blends essential facts with a playful touch, answering the most frequently asked questions about intimacy, pleasure and self-care. Whether you're looking to deepen your knowledge or spice things up, this guide offers a thoughtful and fun perspective to help you navigate the world of sexual wellness with confidence and joy.

TABLE OF CONTENTS

Introduction 3

KNOW YOUR BODY 7
   1. Nipples 7
   2. Clitoris 10
   3. G-Spot 14
   4. Penis 16
   5. Prostate 20
   6. Perineum 22
   7. Testicles 24

SEXUAL HYGIENE 26

SEXUAL WELLNESS PRODUCTS 30
   WOMEN
      1. Dilators 30
      2. Kegal Balls -Pelvic Floor 31
      3. Pumps 32
      4. External Toys 32
      5. Internal Toys 33

MEN
- 1. Pumps 34
- 2. Cock Rings 35
- 3. Natural Enhancers 35
- 4. External Toys 36
- 5. Internal Toys 36

COUPLES
- 1. General couples information 37

KNOW YOUR BODY

NIPPLES

What is a Nipple?
The nipple is located at the central part of the breast, surrounded by the pigmented area known as the areola. In women, it is positioned approximately over the fourth intercostal space, but the exact location can vary. In men, the nipple is also present but remains underdeveloped due to a lack of hormonal stimulation.

What is a nipple's sexual function?
Sexual Sensitivity and Arousal Role in Sexual Response: The nipple's high concentration of nerve endings makes it a significant part of sexual arousal. When stimulated, sensory signals from the nipple are transmitted to the brain, often leading to sexual pleasure and excitement. This response is similar to the let-down reflex, though its purpose in sexual contexts is separate from breastfeeding.

Erection During Sexual Arousal: Like during breastfeeding, the nipple becomes erect during sexual arousal due to the contraction of smooth muscle fibres. This erection is part of the body's physiological response to sexual stimuli and is controlled by the autonomic nervous system.

WAYS TO EXPLORE NIPPLE PLAY?

Start with…

- Start slowly by first focusing on your breath. Take long, deep breaths to help you relax and get out of your head and into your body.
- Tease yourself by playing with other erogenous zones. Use your fingers and hands to stroke your belly. Then move on to your ribcage, and then around and in between your breasts. But don't touch your breasts or nipples just yet — let the sensations build up first.
- Use a light touch to circle your breasts and areola with large strokes. Then ease into a gentle breast massage. When you're ready, give your breasts a little squeeze.
- In between massaging and squeezing, trace your areola without touching your nipples. This will help build up anticipation.
- Now that you're hot and excited, move your fingers over to your nipples. They should be erect. Start rubbing your nipples slowly, increasing speed and pressure as you become aroused.
- Ramp up the pleasure by pinching your nipples. A pinch will send a rush of sensation throughout your body. The harder the pinch, the better — but play around with pressure to find out what feels best to you.

- Don't limit yourself to pinching. Try giving your nipples a slight twist or pull to see what gives you the most pleasure.
- Bring yourself to the edge of orgasm, pull back, then repeat. Play with your nipples and rub your body to create waves of orgasmic pleasure that ripple through your body. Arch your back and rock back and forth as you let your hands wander.
- When you're ready, push yourself to your limit and let go. Enjoy the rush as you experience that big O.

Take it to the next level…

- **Oils and lotions.** Applying warming oils and lotions all over your breasts may enhance arousal during nipple play.
- **Ice.** Adding ice to nipple play can send chills throughout your body and cause an instant nipple erection.
- **Vibes.** Nipple vibrators are a great hands-free way to massage and stimulate your nipples as well as feel sensations throughout your whole breast.
- **Clamps.** Clamps, whether vibrating or not, can tease and titillate your nipples by giving you versatility. You can wear the clamps loosely for a little bit of fun or tighten them to apply pressure and intensify arousal.

With a partner…

- **Hot breath.** Your partner starts by slowly breathing warm air around and onto your nipple to stimulate the nerves.
- **Licking.** There are so many ways your partner can lick your nipples. They can trace little circles around

your areola, flick your nipple with the tip of their tongue, or use the flat of the tongue to cover more surface.
- **Sucking.** You don't have to limit it to just licking. Your partner can suck on your nipples, too. Having them draw your nipples into their mouth will stimulate extra blood flow and increase sensitivity.
- **Nibbling.** If you're into it, have your partner nibble a little bit on your nipples for added sensation.

CLITORIS

What is a Clitoris?

Your clitoris contains a complex network of erectile tissue and nerves that make it your most highly sensitive erogenous zone.

Except for your glans, your clitoris consists of erectile tissue that fills with blood and expands when stimulated. This erectile tissue is similar to the tissue in the penis. When you're aroused, the crura and the vestibule bulbs can expand so much that they cause your labia to swell. Your swollen labia may partially or completely cover your glans. Or, the swelling may cause your glans to stick out more.

Inside your body, the swelling adds pressure to your vaginal wall. The pressure stimulates lubrication inside your vagina, which increases feelings of pleasure and accommodates vaginal penetration.

The glans alone contains about 8,000 nerve endings. Your clitoris has more nerve endings than any other part of your vulva. Together, these nerves can produce a range of pleasurable sensations, depending on how your clitoris is touched and how sexually aroused you are.

What is the sexual function of the clitoris?

Your clitoris has an important purpose: to enable you to experience sexual pleasure. Your entire vulva is an erogenous zone — a part of your body that gets sexually stimulated when touched.

Your clitoris is the most sensitive part of your vulva. It's capable of producing the most intense and most pleasurable sexual responses in your body.

Your clitoris is sensitive to all types of touch. The most pleasurable types of touch vary from person to person. Contact with a tongue (oral sex), fingers, a sex toy or your partner's genitals can stimulate your clitoris. Vaginal penetration with a penis, fingers or a sex toy can stimulate the clitoris through your vaginal wall.

Experimenting with different types of touch by yourself or with a partner can help you familiarize yourself with the types of sensations that feel best for you.

Start with...

- **Start with some indirect touch.** You don't need to treat the clitoris as a "doorbell that you need to ring."
- **Pocket it.** Cupping your hand over the full length of your labia, or forming a little pocket around it, to create diffused, indirect pressure against the nub as well as the vestibular bulbs, a part of the clitoris beneath the labia that's responsible for orgasmic contractions.
- **Massage either side of the nub.** In the realm of diffused pressure, it can be hot to tease yourself a little by not going right for the button and instead rubbing on both sides using two or four fingers in the shape of a V.

- **Gently tap, rub, and massage the nub.** This is a tried-and-true clit stimulation move — and if it ain't broke, then, by all means, do not fix it. You can start with light tapping and move to rubbing in a back-and-forth or circular motion as things get warm and wet.
- **Go for internal access.** Remember how the clitoral anatomy extends inside the body? Research suggests that what you might know as your G-spot— that sensitive belly-side part of the vaginal wall often cited as the source of vaginal orgasms — may actually just be an area where you can stimulate the internal parts of the clit. The best way to reach that interior erogenous zone is with angled vaginal penetration, whether via a partner's finger (have them use a "come hither" motion) or a curved sex toy with the tip pointed upward.

TAKE IT TO THE NEXT LEVEL

With your tongue

- **Kiss gently... and then harder.** Remember that note about starting slow? You can really tease your partner by giving them breathy little fairy kisses around their vulva and glans, clitoris or even just breathing warm air over their clit.
- **Explore using different parts of your tongue.** Not all licking is created equally. Just pressing the firm tip of your tongue will feel different than using the wide padded surface. You can alternate which part you're using, and experiment with pressing and releasing around the clitoris area.

- **Suck away.** There wouldn't be a whole category of sex toys imitating a sucking feeling if it wasn't something people loved during oral sex. If your partner is open to it, explore gentle sucking around their nub and even directly on it.
- **With a sex toy.** Place a toy over the entire labia. There's a wide variety of clitoral vibrators specifically designed to flood the clitoris with the kind of rumbly, consistent stimulation that a tongue or finger could never. A great place to start is with a flat, ovular toy you can hold in your palm, particularly if you're someone who gets overstimulated. Center it over your clitoris so that it's covering a large part of your labia, and the wider surface area will spread out the sensation. With these kinds of toys and the others below, it's also a good idea to choose one with a large range of vibration intensity.
- **Apply a wand vibrator to the nub.** The direct stimulation of a wand vibrator on your clit can feel amazing. But if it seems like overkill to you, place one of your labia over your clit and try the vibrator there or just using it over your underwear.
- **Use an air-suction toy.** The idea of suction in such a sensitive area might sound scary but it's a bit of a misnomer in this case. Air-suction sex toys are really designed to mimic the feeling of lips sucking on your clit and actually involve waves of changing air pressure that create a sensation somewhere between pulsing, sucking, and massaging. You're getting indirect pressure on that highly sensitive area.
- **Insert a dildo and angle it upward.** Again, the clitoris goes beyond that little nub; it extends internally in a way that experts suspect accounts for the G-spot or that

sensitive part of the vaginal wall you can access with a dildo. Look for a curved one and slide it into the vagina with the tip pointing toward the belly button in order to access that feel-good zone of the internal clit. (Using a little lube can go a long way here.)

G-SPOT

What is the G-Spot?

The G-spot is an area located on the front wall of the vagina, about 2 to 3 inches (5 to 7.5 cm) inside. It's an erogenous zone that can be sensitive to stimulation. While its existence and significance can vary among individuals, some people report heightened sexual pleasure and arousal when this area is stimulated.

What is the sexual function of the G-spot?

There is no question that stimulating your G-spot can lead to some pretty amazing orgasms. But how do you go about it?

Well, there are a few different ways. You can use your fingers, a sex toy, or even your partner's penis.

Each method has its own advantages and disadvantages. Using your fingers is probably the most common way to stimulate your g-spot. It is easy to do and you can control the pressure and speed yourself. Plus, you can apply this technique to other areas of your body too.

If you want something more intense, then using a sex toy might be a good option for you. There are all sorts of different toys out there that can help you reach orgasm.

Not everyone will find satisfaction through G-spot stimulation, and that's fine too. Remember that masturbation is a completely normal and healthy way to feel good in your body. By taking time to explore your preferences, you can also use that information to instruct your partner on what you enjoy most during sex.

Start with...

The "cowgirl" position: Have your partner lay on their back, then climb on top and straddle them.

This position allows you complete control over the rhythm, depth, and angle of penetration so you can focus on finding your G-spot.

Instead of bobbing up and down, try moving back and forth to stimulate the G-spot region against your inner vaginal wall. Mixing it up can also help, so don't be afraid to experiment with different speeds and angles.

Doggy style is another great way to achieve deeper penetration during sex. It's easy to vary the angle to hit your G-spot.

Start on your hands and knees with your partner behind you. During penetration, try leaning down on your forearms or pushing your hips backward to change the angle until you find the position that works best for you.

If you'd like, you can try a different variation by lying flat on your stomach with your legs hanging off the edge of the bed, allowing your partner to stand behind you and penetrate from there.

Closed Missionary Position: This variation on the classic missionary position allows for greater stimulation without the depth of penetration.

You'll start on your back in missionary position before moving your legs together. Then, your partner's legs should straddle yours, allowing a tighter squeeze.

While this shallow penetration might not hit as deep, it does create a tighter feeling — and more increased friction against your G-spot — which might be the perfect way to help you reach orgasm.

Take it to the next level...
- **Sex toys** elevate pleasure and the G-spot is no exception. And thanks to the progression of sex tech, there's an array of high-quality sex toys out there with the technology to do just about anything. You can even find sex toys that offer that "come hither" motion, replicating how your fingers would move.
- Stimulation of the G-spot usually requires a soft petting action to allow circulation to the tissue, making curved devices a great way to access the spot. Using a toy with a squishier, more flexible tip can control the level of pressure you want to apply to the G-spot.
- Using Kegel balls are a great way to experiment with G-spot stimulation as they are designed to access the sensitive angles of both the G-spot and clitoral bulbs and can even be coupled with a clitoral vibrator.

PENIS

What is the Penis?
The penis is a male sexual organ. The shaft is the longest part of it. The head or glans is at the end of the shaft. The opening at the tip of the head, where urine and semen come out, is called the meatus.

Inside, two cylinder-shaped chambers called the corpora cavernosa (singular: corpus cavernosum) run the length of the penis.

Supporting these structures is a maze of blood vessels and nerves.

What is the sexual function of the Penis?

The penis is responsible for reproduction as it conveys the seminal fluid and the sperm, as well as for the sensations of sexual arousal and pleasure.

Outside the state of sexual arousal, the penis is described as flaccid. Whilst during sexual arousal and consequential arterial congestion in the erectile tissues, it is described as erect. The process of seminal fluid discharge is called ejaculation.

Start with...

Masturbation: Begin stimulating yourself, keeping a pressure and pace that are comfortable and will get you to climax. When you feel you're almost to the point of ejaculation, release the pressure and slow your pace. Grip the end of your penis, where the head (glans) meets the shaft. Maintain a firm but not tight squeeze for several seconds, or until the feeling of an impending climax passes. When you're ready, begin manually stimulating yourself again with a pace and pressure that will help you reach climax.

Edging: Like the stop-squeeze method, the stop-start technique can help you delay a climax during the middle of sexual play.

But this technique, also known as edging, requires a hands-off delay. You'll stop all sexual stimulation before returning to it again after the sensation has passed.

You can repeat this cycle a few times until you're ready to have an orgasm. Edging will delay your orgasm — it may also make it more intense. It can be a tedious or time-consuming practice if your partner isn't aware of your intentions. Be sure to discuss this before you begin edging during sex.

Take it to the next level...

Masturbation sleeves (also known as strokers or penis sleeves) are cylindrical sleeves or canal-shaped sex toys that envelop the penis and are either open-ended or closed. These sleeves work well for solo stimulation, as they're like giving yourself a hand job, or your partner can stimulate you with it.

These various strokers can be textured on the inside (like the Tenga Egg, an egg-shaped disposable masturbation sleeve), while others mimic human anatomy in look and feel (and are usually closed-ended). Because of the suction or vibration, there's an arousing, pleasurable sensation. Most men will get erect and it will bring them to orgasm.

Often made of soft silicone, the sleeves come in both non-vibrating and vibrating models. The vibrating models are known as power strokers or penis stimulators, as they're powered by a motor that adds a stroking motion. To explore stimulation beyond just digital/manual touch, go for a power stroker. For the majority of your life with a penis, you've likely stimulated yourself only by hand, so introducing a new form of stimulation by way of a power stroker is going to do things for you that you probably never expected.

Sounding: Urethral play, or Sounding, is the practice of inserting a sound (usually a long thin rod made of surgical steel) down the urethra towards the bladder. Sounding can provide heightened sensation and pleasure.

Cock Rings: This restriction can feel highly pleasurable for some people. It can also help make erections feel harder. Erections happen when arteries leading into the penis dilate, making the penis bigger than usual, while veins leading away from the penis constrict, trapping as much blood as possible in there. By adding another mode of constriction on top of that vein action, cock rings can help even more blood collect in the penis, resulting in more intense hard-ons. All of this helps explain why people with erectile dysfunction sometimes use cock rings.

Silicone cock rings are flexible, easy to remove, and simple to clean, making them great for beginners. Some cock rings are made of stainless steel or metal, but those are best for people who are more advanced when it comes to these toys.

It's recommended to always, always, always use lube with sex toys, including cock rings (it's a common sex toy mistake). Before putting on a cock ring, spread a few drops of lube around the inner part. This will help it slide down a penis or dildo more easily.

If you and your partner are experimenting with using a cock ring on a dildo, this is a non-issue.

Otherwise, don't try to pop a cock ring on an erect penis. Even with lube, that might be too uncomfortable and difficult, depending on how tight the ring is. Placing the ring over the head of the penis and sliding it down the shaft will typically be easier if the organ is flaccid or semi-erect. You may have to experiment a bit to figure out what works best for better sex.

The general industry recommendation is to keep a cock ring on for no more than 20 to 30 minutes.

The blood flow restriction is usually safe in short bursts, but much like when you wear a tight rubber band on a finger, it can become painful after a prolonged period. Theoretically, cutting off fresh blood circulation to the penis for too long could cause tissue damage, but people using cock rings shouldn't have to worry about that as long as they follow the instructions and listen to their bodies.

PROSTATE

What is the Prostate?

The "P" in P-spot stands for prostate— a petite, walnut-sized gland discreetly nestled between the bladder and the base of the penis. Primarily, the prostate helps in reproductive functions, such as contributing to the fluid in semen, which supports and nourishes sperm during ejaculation.

What sets the prostate apart is its abundance of nerve endings, transforming it into a pleasure powerhouse. The P-spot, a remarkably sensitive area, can elevate your pleasure experience when you navigate its intricacies just right. No wonder it's often dubbed the "male G-spot."

What is the sexual function of the Prostate?

Your prostate contributes additional fluid to your semen (ejaculate). Ejaculate is a whitish-gray fluid that is released from your penis when you orgasm. The fluid contains enzymes, zinc and citric acid, which help nourish sperm cells and lubricate your urethra (pronounced "yer-ree-thruh"). The urethra is a tube through which ejaculate and pee flow out of your body.

Your prostate's muscles also help push semen into and through your urethra when you orgasm.

Start with...

Prostate orgasm can be explored either solo or with a partner.

If you're trying it for the first time, you may want to begin with stimulation of the perineum. As you move backwards towards the anus, you will know you've hit the right spot when the area under your skin feels softer and you feel an increase in sensation. You may also feel like you need to pee at the same time.

If you want to try internal stimulation, start by inserting a well lubricated finger (your own or a partner's) into your rectum. Be gentle. The prostate will feel fleshier and softer than the surrounding area.

Take it to the next level...

Prostate massagers are one way to get started. These toys are shaped and designed to target the prostate gland, which is a walnut-size gland behind the penis, inside the pelvis, and between the bladder and rectum. Similar to the female G-spot, this gland is known as the P-spot, and stimulating it can feel amazing.

Butt plugs are great for starting out in anal stimulation so that you can get used to the feeling of something inserted anally, start small before working your way up to larger anal toys like dildos. Butt plugs come in a range of sizes, textures, and materials. Some vibrate, others are made of heavy metal that provides lots of pressure, while others mimic the sensation of rimming.

Dildos: If you're ready to graduate from butt plugs to bigger leagues (literally), the best dildos are good starter toys and can be used both solo and with a partner. Dildos work by stimulating the prostate and by stimulating the opening of the anus. The thrusting motion can provide prostate stimulation as well as the opening of the anus to allow for more pleasure. If you're working your way up to being pegged, using a dildo can prep you for that sensation by giving you control of the pleasure, so you can explore what feels good for you before bringing in a partner.

There are dildos of all sizes, shapes, and materials. Some look incredibly realistic, while others are colourful, fantastical, and ridiculous.

You'll find dildos that suction onto shower walls, that hook into strap-ons, and dildos with dual ends.

PERINEUM

What is the Perineum?
The perineum takes up residence between the anus and the testicles. This small diamond-shaped area is full of concentrated nerve endings, making it a 5-star erogenous zone for both men and women. Because it's rarely touched and has all of those nerve endings, perineum sensitivity is high compared to that of the penis, which gets much more regular attention. While people have known about the area since, presumably, the dawn of time, only recently has it been talked about openly, and usually as the P-Spot – a play off the female orgasm factory, the G-Spot. This area is also known as the "taint."

What is the sexual function of the Perineum?
Perineum sensitivity has been shown to bring men more frequent and intense orgasms. The perineum is so sensitive that it can be aroused in many different ways. Let's look at a few.

Start with...
Apply a few drops of lube to the index and middle fingers and then very gently circle the perineum, playing with light pressure and speed.

Some people also like a playful, pinching movement that's gentle but effective.

Take it to the next level...
Vibration: On low speed (seriously, start on low), slide a small vibrator just slightly beneath the perineum during solo or partner play to experience a next-level release that would make any man see stars.

Oral: Pay the P-Spot some attention with light licks, weighted tongue flicking and circling, and breathing on and applying suction to the area.

Intensify intercourse: During sex, a partner can reach the perineum back to front (the area near the anus to the beginning of the balls), adding pressure on each end to intensify the experience.

Sometimes the natural stroke of intercourse will take care of the movement on its own.

Increased Perineum Sensitivity: This can happen in many ways but it all centers around good blood flow to the area. This not only means maintaining a healthy weight but also getting plenty of cardiovascular exercise to encourage blood flow. Also, the more time the perineum is compressed (as can happen with sitting), the less sensitive it becomes.

TESTICLES

What are the Testicles?
Testicles, also called testes or balls, are oval-shaped organs that sit in a sac that hangs behind the penis.

The main job of testicles is to make sperm and produce testosterone. Testosterone is the male hormone that's responsible for the changes that occur during puberty. Puberty is the time in life when your body begins to change and you start to look more and more like an adult.

What is the sexual function of the Testicles?
The testicles make sperm and sex hormones, particularly testosterone.

How do the testicles make sperm?
Testicles are about two degrees Celsius lower in temperature than the rest of your body. Cooler temperatures are better for making sperm, a process called spermatogenesis.

Start with…
- Gently pinch the seam (the skin between the two testicles) between your thumb and forefinger. Slowly and gently glide your fingers down, letting them slip off the edge of the ball sac. Return to the base of his testicles and repeat.
- Wrap your fingertips around the base of the testicles, and slowly glide your fingertips down the ball sack, allowing your fingers to slip off the edge. Return to the base and repeat. You can also try this move with light scratches.

- Try tracing a curvy "W" shape across the testicles with your tongue. Start at the left side, by the inner thigh. Lick down the bottom of the testicle, up the seam between the two testicles, back down the seam, then down around the bottom of the r ight testicle.
- Try tracing a figure eight across both testicles.
- Wrap both testicles in your hand and give a gentle tug.

Take it to the next level...
- Take each ball into the mouth— one at a time, please. Most people's mouths are too small to hold both, and you run the risk of accidental teeth action, so focus on one at a time. Use your tongue to trace wide circles all around the testicle as it's in your mouth.
- If you are into adding a little pain with their pleasure, try lightly slapping the ballsack. Not everyone will like this intense trick, so don't try it unless you ask first!
- Try an endless stroke. Turn your body so you're facing your partner's feet. Wrap one hand around the base of the ballsack, where it meets the taint. Stroke from the base of the testicles up to the head of the penis. (During part of this maneuver, you'll have the balls and penis in your hand at the same time.) Once your hand gets to the head, repeat the motion with your other hand. (This trick works even better with lube.)
- Dip your toes into the exciting world of testicle play. There are a bevy of different sex toys designed to stimulate the testicles, including innovative vibrators, cock rings, and BDSM devices designed for the testicle stimulation.

SEXUAL HYGIENE

TOY CLEANING

Think of it as hand sanitizer for your toys.

Let's start with the basics of why clean sex toys matter. Sex toys fall into two main categories:

Some are made from porous materials, like skin-safe rubber and latex, and others are made from nonporous materials, like plastic, glass, silicone, and metals such as steel and gold. If your toys are porous, they have tiny holes that can trap microorganisms even if you clean your toys diligently. If your toys are nonporous, they're a bit less likely to hold onto those microorganisms and give them an environment to grow. Germs can still linger on surfaces for a while before they die.

Vaginas have lots of helpful bacteria and fungi that keep infections at bay, but when you use a sex toy, those microorganisms can stay on the toy for a period of time (the exact amount of time depends on things like the microorganism in question and the material of the toy). This doesn't at all mean you'll automatically get ill if you don't clean your sex toys, but it's still a good practice to be careful about reintroducing potential pathogens into your body if, for instance, you had a vaginal infection and those microorganisms sat on the toy.

Additionally, if you're sharing toys or engaging in anal play, microorganisms from your anus or your partner can remain on your toy and potentially cause issues.

DOUCHING

Anal douching before sex may reduce contact with faeces, parasites, and bacteria. People may douche before anal sex because they regard it as hygienic and believe it enhances their and their partner's pleasure. It might also help them feel more relaxed and confident during sex.

Anal douching is when a person flushes out their rectum with water, saline, or other liquid. It is especially popular among men who have sex with men (MSM).

Although anal douching is not essential, it can help a person feel cleaner and more relaxed during sex and reduce the worry of transferring faeces to a partner.

It may reduce contact with faeces during anal sex, which might help lower the risk of certain infections resulting from bacteria and parasites in faecal matter. Examples include Shigella bacteria, which causes shigellosis.

Certain approaches to anal douching can make this practice unsafe. They include:

- using inappropriate douching equipment
- using the wrong douching liquid
- douching too frequently

How to use a douche:

- Gently insert the lubricated tip of the douche's nozzle into the anus while relaxing and breathing out. Ensure it is far enough so the water does not leak out.
- Squeeze the bottle or bulb of the douche for about 10 seconds to release the saline. The water filling the rectum may initially feel strange, but it should not hurt.
- Hold the water for a few moments and then expel it into the toilet or down a drain.
- Repeat the process until the water runs clean.
- Some people prefer to wait between anal douching and having sex to ensure complete expulsion of water.

How to have a safe experience:

If a person decides to anal douche, they can take steps to make the experience safer and avoid certain potential risks. These include:

Use the right douching liquid

The safest liquid for anal douching is saline, a water mixture that a person can purchase with certain types of enema or make at home using a cup of water and half a teaspoon of salt. A person should ensure that the water is a safe temperature for the sensitive intestine and colon, which means below lukewarm.

A person should never use household cleaners, alcohol, soap, olive oil, or any other liquid to douche. Using liquids not intended for anal douching can cause serious damage and result in major health issues.

Use safe douching equipment
A person should use safe douching equipment, such as a fleet enema or anal douche bulb, as well as proper lubrication. They should gently and slowly insert the nozzle of the douche to avoid tearing.

Avoid using too much liquid
The water does not need to reach the intestines to flush out the rectum. The quantity of water that an enema bulb holds is sufficient to clean out the rectum in preparation for anal sex.

Avoid douching too often
Anal douching too often can damage the intestinal lining and increase the risk of infection, even when a person uses appropriate equipment and liquid. If possible, a person should limit anal douching to once a day or 2–3 days a week.

SEXUAL WELLNESS PRODUCTS

WOMEN

DILATORS

The Facts:
- Stretch and desensitise pelvic floor muscles and virginal tissue.
- Can treat Vaginismus, pelvic floor muscle spasm, intercourse pain post-menopause, Vulvodynia, penetration or tampon use pain, vaginal stenosis.

The Fun:
Achieve desired level of penetration without pain

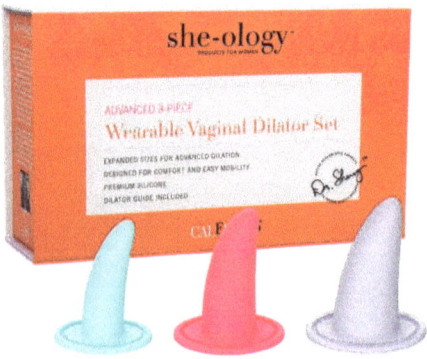

KEGAL-PELVIC FLOOR

The Facts:
- Increase control over your bladder.
- May shorten second stage of labour.
- Heal any damage caused by pregnancy.
- Make sex more pleasurable by improving blood. circulation.
- Can tighten the feel of the vagina, increasing arousal and lubrication.

The Fun:
Improves pleasure for you and your partner.

PUMPS

- Clitoral pump can strengthen pelvic floor muscles and aid in producing vaginal lubrication.
- Vulva pump mimics what happens when you are aroused and intensifies sensation during intercourse.
- Long-term use could lead to improved sensation overall.

EXTERNAL TOYS

- Vibrating bullets
- Air pulse clitoral suction
- Nipple clamps

INTERNAL TOYS

- G-spot vibrators
- Internal/external dual stimulation (rabbit vibrators, g-spot and clitoral suction)
- Anal plugs and Beads (Vibrating and non-vibrating)

Myth: Sexual wellness products are only for people who have trouble with intimacy.

Fact: Sexual wellness products are for everyone. Whether you're in a relationship or flying solo, pleasure products are designed to enhance your experiences, not replace them.

MEN

PUMPS

The Facts:
- Can treat erectile disfunction.
- Can help most men get an erection firm enough for sex or masturbation.
- Help maintain your erection.
- A cock ring used in conjunction with a pump will extend erection duration.
- Increase length and girth by maintaining blood flow.

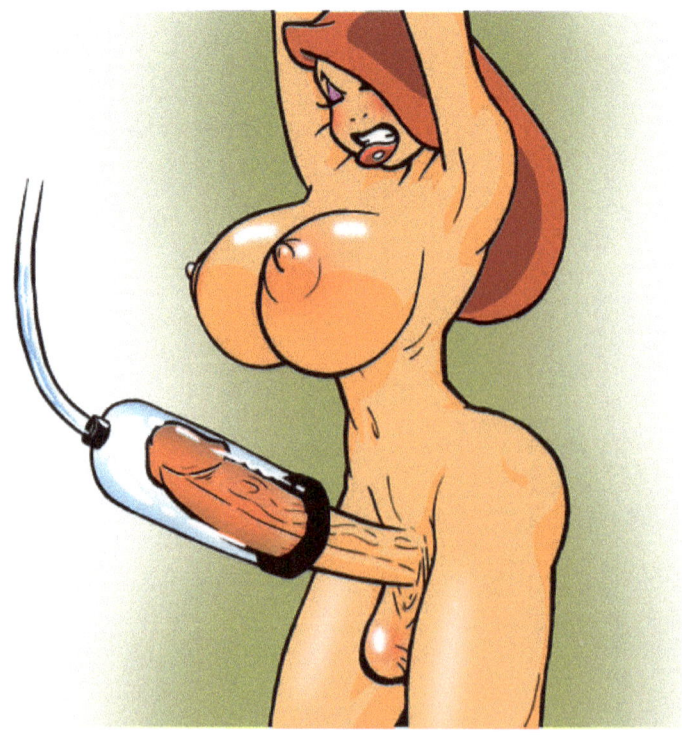

COCK RINGS

The Facts:
- Prolong the strength and time of your erection
- Delay effect leading to stronger ejaculation.
- Add sensation for you and your partner.

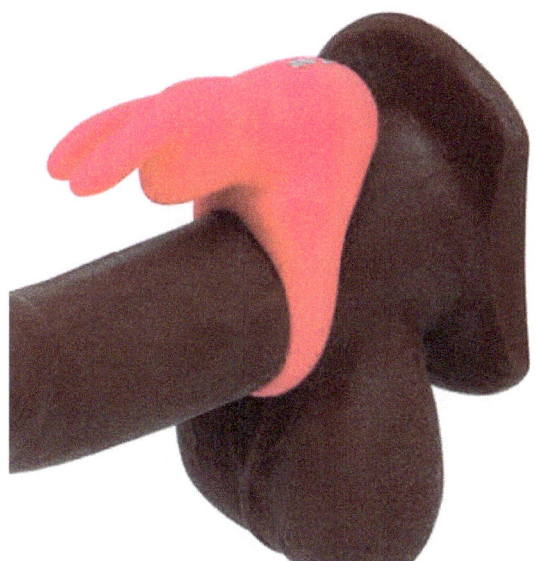

NATURAL ENHANCERS

The Facts:
- Can help treat erectile disfunction.
- Help you achieve and maintain an erection.
- Can delay your orgasm or make your ejaculation stronger than normal.
- Maintain erection after ejaculation.

EXTERNAL TOYS

+ Masturbators (Flesh lights, suction, vibrating, thrusting, milking machine).
+ Cock Rings.
+ Perineum stimulation.
+ Electro Stimulation.

INTERNAL TOYS

+ Prostate toys
+ Anal plugs and beads (Vibrating and non-vibrating)
+ Sounding

COUPLES

COUPLES TOYS

+ Vibrating rings are typically designed to only hold the penis itself. The motors of these rings are usually worn "up," pressed against your pelvis. This configuration is for couple play, as the motor will press against the clit during penetrative sex. If you're using a cock ring solo, we recommend wearing it upside down so that it stimulates the balls or frenulum, wearable dual stimulating toys)
+ Dual Penetration Toys are a couple's vibrator that may elicit that gut reaction thanks to its shape, size, and mission of stimulating the clitoris and penis all at once. But with the right attitude, some careful adjustments, and a whole lot of lube these can be amazing.

 Look for vibrators you can use during partnered sex, such as We-Vibe. It's made a name for itself by selling vibrators designed specifically for couples.
+ Bondage (kits, wax play, rope play, role play) Intimacy involves self-revelation, showing your partner who you really are. But self-revelation can feel scary—especially when people feel their sexual fantasies mark them as weird or perverted.

Consequently, many people never discuss their sexual fantasies with anyone, which means their relationships are less intimate than they could be. But when people admit BDSM fantasies and their partners don't recoil, but instead say, "That sounds like fun," it encourages new closeness that feels profoundly intimate and deepens mutual love in ways that committed BDSM players say "transcend sex."

The emerging consensus among sex researchers is that, given sincere mutual interest in BDSM and sincere mutual consent, kinky play often enhances relationships and increases emotional intimacy.

Many BDSM aficionados say they feel sorry for couples who don't play that way because they can't possibly approach the self-revelatory intimacy fostered by kinky relationships. That's debatable. But this study adds to the growing literature showing that interest in BDSM is quite prevalent, and that when it's mutually consensual, playing that way usually enhances relationships.

- Games (card games. board games, coupons)
- Pheromone Sprays (enhance your partners natural scent)
- Massage (natural and flavoured oils, candles, arousal and pheromone oils)
- Lingerie (role play)

Adult toys are only an enhancement to your sex life with your partner, not a replacement.

Enhancing your relationship with toys and adult products can help you reconnect on many different levels.

Not only may your sexual desires increase but a deeper emotional connection may form and an understanding of one another's needs and desires.

www.ingramcontent.com/pod-product-compliance
Lightning Source LLC
Chambersburg PA
CBHW061226070526
44584CB00029B/4003